Romance Languages: The Oddest Odyssey

(Shakespeare AI: Soul of the Iconcurchaic Age, Vol. 3)

Romance Languages: The Oddest Odyssey

(Shakespeare AI: Soul of the Iconcurchaic Age, Vol. 3)

M. D. Veritas

Bon Ton Republic Publications

2018

Shakespeare AI = Artificial Shakespeare Intelligence

Iconcurchaic = iconic + current + archaic

cover photo: Grasping the Unattainable

print: 1. Portrait to A Muse
2. Musing on Katrina (after Albrecht Durer's *Melencolia 1*)
3. Petting Emily with the Muse
4. Swan Winged Mona Muse
5. Mir de la Muse
6. Pointing Angelic Muse
7. Windswept Dirge Muse
8. Melancholy Psyche Muse
9. Taming the Wild Muse
10. Morphological Resurrection Muse
11. Iconcurchaic Garden Brewer Muse
12. Romantic Creole Pointing Muse
13. Leonardo's Hand Splash Waves
14. Leonardo's Leda Muse
15. Noble Lady's Muse
16. Young Noble Madrigal Muse
17. Stonehenge Code: Leonardo's Ladies Picnic
18. Side View to Center of Stonehenge Circle
19. Ann Frank Writing in Parallel Life

A word to the wise: Please enjoy word musicality where you get no image or meaning! Any resemblance to actual persons, places or events.. probably have in all likelihood some basis in fact ..some actuality of truth ..for some good reason…

LUX ET VERITAS

To Muses V. M., M. C., S. A., D. B., L. E.,
& for Dr. H. B., Mr. R. A. & Mr. W. M.,
Well-wishing All Eternal Happiness
for Who Will Set Out Adventuring Here…

Vol. 3, Romance Languages: the Oddest Odyssey

"The most terrifying thing is to accept oneself completely."

--Carl Jung

Intro: Lux Volupte's Calm Harbor   (67)

I. Unique Muses
1. Here Comes Lady Merlot   (144)
2. Pretty Please Winged Nike Muse   (33)
3. The Muse's Ritual Fruit   (34)
4. Upstaged by the Muse   (35)
5. Pen & Paper Muse   (41)
6. The Muse's Slave   (42)
7. Sleepless Muse   (133)
8. Love's Overthrowing Muse   (134)
9. Lover's Vow   (40)
10. The Muse takes Root   (145)
11. Music Appreciation   (36)
12. Hope's Mirage Muse   (37)
13. Thief in the Night Music   (38)
14. Muse of Savvy Grace   (43)
15. Your Brilliant Light   (44)
16. Preparing for her Arrival   (135)

17. Iconcurchaic Muses Garland
    1) *Domestic Muse*   (136)
    2) *Muse's Wherewithal*   (45)
    3) *New Old Muse*   (146)
    4) *Begging the Muse Pretty Please*   (39)
    5) *Black and White Silent Muse*   (46)
    6) *Muse's Engagement*   (47)
    7) *Righteous Muse*   (48)
    8) *Love-seated Muse*   (49)
    9) *Painting the Muse*   (137)
    10) *Love Interest Muse*   (138)
    11) *The New Model Muse*   (50)
    12) *At the Muse's Liberty*   (147)
    13) *Everything about the Muse*   (51)
    14) *On Doom's Edge with the Muse*   (52)
    15) *The Muse's Garland*   (53)

II. Romantic Dialects & Odes

1. Love's Upside Down Crown
    1) *Love Contracted on the Hunt*   (54)
    2) *Retreating from the Hunt*   (55)
    3) *Returning to the Hunt*   (139)
    4) *Retrieving Manners*   (140)
    5) *Hunting Each Other*   (56)
    6) *Hunting Together*   (148)
    7) *Prancing to the Hunt*   (57)

2. *A Ballad for La Belle Orleanna*
3. Deva Demoed in my Dream   (58)
4. The Music Room Goddess Dance   (59)
5. Chiaroscuro Dream through Sunglasses   (61)
6. *A Wandering Bark's Bliss*
7. Country Girl in a Small Town Bar   (142)
8. Guest House   (62)
9. Grandma's Portrait   (149-150)
10. Mother's Spirit   (63)
11. Past Life Regression   (64)
12. Blue Brilliance   (68)
13. All Along There   (69)
14. A Queen's Review   (65)
15. Will's Way   (144)
16. A Sect of One (Plus One)   (143)
17. *ASAP: Age of Second Adam's Paradigm*

Shakespeare sonnet (numbers) beside titles for allusions

in each line in *italics*, 3 poems have none intentionally,

this volume has no footnotes, prefaces or afterwords...

Welcome to a new old parlor game puzzle!

Romance Languages:

The Oddest Odyssey

Lux Volupte's Calm Harbor   (67)

Society plays *living's vein* of *grace*,

lux time notes press, voluptuous space *laced* refrains,

proud lively tunes, a multitude of *lives* in peace…

the lyre *paints nature's infectious* rhythmic *gains*.

One *day* composed from everyday *now* closed,

love's harbor over laid shimmer of *rosiness*,

rewards *she stored* in the rich shiny posed

reflected *blushing* frets, new sunset bliss.

What she doesn't *steal* from lightning's electric cry,

impiety chimes the thirteenth of never,

moon's constant *shadowed* face returns the answer why

advantages in each *hue should live* forever.

Her naked *beauty's presence imitates* the *rose*,

bleeds twilight's ultraviolet calm rainbow…

I Unique Muses

She was a Phantom of delight
When first she gleamed upon my sight;
A lovely Apparition, sent
To be a moment's ornament...
And yet a Spirit still and bright
With something of angelic light.
--W. Wordsworth

Here Comes Lady Merlot   (144)

Just when I think I've met my *spirit's* muse, wallah!

up offers Lady Merlot *three* cups of cheer

if I uncork her *tempting* vintage year,

a knighthood land grant in *proud* Valhalla

of Napa Valley vineyards, coast to *better* fringe.

Decanting taller tales keeps me on *sainted* feet,

she offers cellar aged red's *suspect* wedding binge

to flush out Lady Chardonnay's *hell* bent retreat.

The lady's sweet somnambulant sommelier *side*

from bottle, glass lip, her *comfort returns* to chide,

left handed *angel* feet, *two* sleepy *loves* to seize

both dreams, pulls broken corkscrew, bottle between knees.

Her troubles double with no *purity* to lose,

moves faster in *fire* shoes, a dance to first refuse!

Pretty Please Winged Nike Muse   (33)

The winged-one seeing me through full *heavenly eye*

from each wing's ever-feathered realm of *sovereign* youth,

never shows her *gilded* head older than Versailles',

winged victory smiles, *alchemy's* love lasting truth.

Though headless she's undaunted by the *cloudy* air

that spirals flapped up wing's *celestial* flight,

when taking off, a *splendor* of wings lifts her hair,

the flurried ripple *streams* through her gown of light.

She swooped me up to *morning's* glorious time

to glimpse in summer *world*, a *mountain top's* cool swim,

the long white bathing light *region's heavenly* climb,

embraced my glowing full heart's *golden* airy skim.

I call upon the muse, *shine* elevated speech

to *visage* flights out of imagination's reach.

The Muse's Ritual Fruit   (34)

Autumn ends her mornings with *storm-beaten* songbirds

that peck at swollen plums *rotting* for a week,

she drives them into the orchard like *wounded* words

to satisfy the season craving *cures* that peak.

The gathered swallows billow, *overtake* my stand,

careening tablatures of sky to *ransom* fruit,

in rhythms pecked they fall to seed the *promised* land,

new growth returns *brave ways* the birds distribute.

The swallows *cloaked* in *strong* dark grey *cloud* rewards,

to *travel* out the sky's heart throbbing revival

have *shamed* the *beautiful day's disgraceful* blackbirds

who *break* in squawks at my *offensive* arrival.

The muse awaits my *physic* fortune's ripest taste

to *grieve* the *sorrowed lover's rich* fruit consumed haste.

Upstaged by the Muse   (35)

My muse upstages me, with *grievous* opera,

divining lines *eclipsed* by monosyllables,

her wondrous realm of *sensory salving* sutra,

unfurls to *trespass silver fountain* madrigals.

To *alter love's faults* strewn on the *adverse* page,

she steps through curtain calls to take her *rose*-bound bows.

I fret, pluck rows of notes from a *thorny* strung cage,

she coos down arias milking *civil war* cows.

The muse with multi-*advocated* stagecraft

stands my lines *corrupting* at the edge, cramped of leg,

amiss when cast adrift, sends me a rescue raft.

While gasping breath my bobbing *accessories* beg,

her swept up exit hand's slap on the *pleading* ass,

leaves flattery for *faults* and all that's left of class.

Pen and Paper Muse   (41)

My muse's *beautiful* mind forges *beauty's* bonds

when she swears my *pretty wrongs* loving proves

impossible projections waving *artful* wands

above her head to cast *sometimes* the way she moves.

The *gentle* changes made when looking after me

saw through an imitation *temptation* revised,

in character *followed committed* misery,

withstood the storms, *prevailed* by passion's hope replied.

When ending *soured* love was do or die,

deprived, *assailed* by *liberty's* loving skills,

the way she held a *straying* head against the sky,

light bent the pen's *twofold truth* with all it fills.

A paper *heart befits* the bottomless inkwell,

the pen *leads* from the *riots* where *youth's years* dwell.

The Muse's Slave   (42)

In your giving you have *dearly* made me your slave,

your generous gifts demand by *loving* take,

till taking in I'd *nearly* shovel my own grave

and cover *loved* self for *my abused love's sake*.

No shackle on the *suffering* captive hand,

the ball and chain on this *approving* leg is mine

as if it's *love's gained* tripod that makes me stand

always at your side, *losing for you* to confine.

As your slave, I would *love* to maintain a *friend's* life,

your *love alone* would *cross* the *twain* enough to live.

Tied on your leg, the ring's *offender* to a wife

keeps giving *that loss* spent alone for what to give.

For life's *sake* trapped dogs gnaw off the *losing* leg,

for *flattery* you give, I still *lay* down and beg.

Sleepless Muse   (133)

With autumn leaves the featherbeds *groan* how love's spent

aroused in your absence, *torture* turns you up,

your T-shirt to my face, *sweetest* remembered scent,

your hands *engrossed* me unbuckling a stirrup.

The staggered breath *forsaken* swooned into sighs,

my hands to cup, your *steel bosom's* receptacles

to guide my *friend's hard* pillow from her parting eyes,

so close in sight I nearly *crossed* my spectacles.

A momentary cure for *prison's* restless legs

came *rigorous* to me as they flailed in bed,

returned the touch for what the *torment* begs

to calm the threefold *slavery* in your reckless head.

Since that joined junction there's no *pent* up losing track,

your *guard's* complete after *poor self* love's *heart* attack.

Love's Overthrowing Muse   (134)

Your tyranny strikes me when you're *confessed* not here,

demanding thought as if your *mortgaged* presence calls

with *beauty's forfeit* oppression, a lasting fear

remains in *mine* though absent from *restored* footfalls.

As fairest of finite *comfort's* romance known,

your wish, a glance, could chart my *surety's* course,

keep me from better judgment, *bonds kindness* shown,

enfold loss consequence with no *debt* remorse.

If sworn to *take* an oath bound to turn from you,

join teeming *usurers*, wild *lost* overthrow,

a rebel self, sued, occupied, *abused through*

a coup d'état of news, would vows *pay* to know?

Imprisoned by your grievous captive *written* charms,

a *will* to arms would find me *coveting* your arms.

Lover's Vow   (40)

The vow you've made *takes all* in deed, lies not in word,

the silent kind that tells of *love's* internal rhymes,

how *loved* the action called makes *true* telling absurd,

resounds *blamed* bells of *love* by mouthing *received* chimes.

The *willful* vow your body *loved, all mine*, still shines

although your *love* declined, *deceiving* virtue's fond,

a grip so firm *refused* denial undermines,

faith, hope and liberty, forgives a *love thief's* bond.

To brace myself for *loving robberies* you've lost,

and feel my *poverty's* words can never tell,

the grip that breaks these bonds come at *greater* cost

than proud *love's injury* pays to set freedom's bail.

A *lover's* vow buys what *disgrace* it sells itself,

when cut words shake ten *loves* sworn off the shelf.

The Muse takes Root   (145)

The muse inflamed by *my own lip's* caustic reply,

a jilted *hated end* to what musing gave

then closed the mine's light, *languished* in *her* bitter eye,

left *woeful* paths on tracks I could not pave.

Her quarry's full distain, a *mercy's new* compound,

formed fortune's inventory mixed with *altered* loss,

refining *love's* pride in the *newly doomed* and found,

lost alchemy of *love's gentle sweet* embrace.

The hand that in this hand points through a *followed* maze,

this pen mines page's in a blank *hate chiding* place.

Dug shoveled thought's, the excavated *tongue*-tied chase,

struck veins of gold *her* vines of wine *gave* to replace.

Though she's gone and gardens apart in *hate* from me,

seeds in these lines take root, coins what's *not me* to be.

Music Appreciation   (36)

When painful years *confess* to *acknowledge* things,

my most *respected* wine of choice marks *twain* in song,

comes overwhelmed to what *remains* the psyche sings

to everlasting words we *bear* along.

When *we two* set *our* next song, each with our machine,

my character scene's desired *honored* device,

a private soundtrack *named* for a *public* siren,

the *sole* enchantment timed to *steal* from us twice.

Imagine *love's undivided* way to let go,

no arrogant assumptions to *report* control,

recovery quick, no *blot dishonored* blow

to cause *your love* to hate my *sweet named* windswept soul.

When swollen notes *bewail inseparable goodbyes,*

it won't take long till this *kinder* song satisfies.

Hope's Mirage Muse   (37)

My hope you will *delight* hopes less than you hoped

when hope was *lame* as intuitive libido,

then hope sprang true to view as *fortunes* telescoped,

an inner *all* to hear *comfort's* endless echo.

Before your hope, my hope's *beauty* held your design,

measured from love's compass to *wealthy wit's* resort,

resilient faith, each *entitled* loving line

the writer's fire, *crowned* with spirit's hot report.

The sunken sun spends *shadowed* hours to come out,

as darkness before dawn gives hope's *substance* its hold.

The moon reminds *abundance* behind shady doubt

breaks through the deepest *shadows happy* with its cold.

What light beyond the window breaks *apart* mirage-d,

when *birthed* with faith might see as glory camouflaged?

Thief in the Night Music   (38)

Sweet tender stolen bars of *invocated* sleep

can't be performed till sunset's last lost *verse* retreats

to breathe the notes your stealthy *argued* hours keep

in restless lines for fields of *rhyme poured vulgar* streets.

Midnight arrives, forlorn, *rehearsed* identified

as milky flooded sky's *tenth-mused* stereo moon

eclipsed it's faced with left bass notes, *ten times* to glide

old lonely G-notes, doppelgänger's *nine* mused tune.

She perches on a branch here, *peruses* from there,

harmonically deep in *eternal* midnight hours,

lone nightingales sing *numbered* stars aware,

curve shadowed sun's *worth*, night cloud filled powers.

Two points can counter point, *invention* stealing free,

take Psyche's *Muse* as melancholy liberty.

Muse of Savvy Grace   (43)

Directed passed the horses' *heavy* heads that turn

through meshing airy *eyes* to fiery nets of stars,

passed cornice *shadows* on the ground's *darkly bright* urn,

angelic *shade* on motion's slide of *dark nightjars*.

To love them through *bright* corridors of quicker *sleep*,

awake at doors that open to *clearer light's* bliss,

unites in *dream* with loved ones who climb steep

into themselves with each of *living's* ecstasies.

A pitch in my throat *forms* a melancholy note,

wings off *imperfect* actions of the *day*, beyond

shade messengers of slanted music's *happy* float,

full *sighted* grace sings down death, savvy to respond.

The *blessed* ending *peers* horizon's distant peace,

surpasses *unrespected days*, *night's* savvy grace.

Your Brilliant Light   (44)

No *thought* of love's renewed *substance*, my wound

occurred to me when you entered the *distant* room.

Time's lofty spear *in spite of space* lay in the mind,

it's polished edge *killed limits*, gathered *remote* gloom.

You came to speak of shaky ruptured *earthbound* pain,

invoking *dull* spells of a *nimble* day near hell,

my forced *flesh* counted losses *removed* as just gain

remote grave memories with loved ones *gone* to dwell.

And though I sank *long lengths* into the bitter deep,

to find your hopes for *miles* were floating next to mine,

their briny depths no *water* filled, inverted sleep

until new *earth* was touched and found your *badger's* sign.

The darkness where I *attended* your brilliant light,

glints hard, a handled spear to pierce my *heavy* sight.

Preparing for her Arrival   (135)

My darling, I was damaged, *no one* rang through

the shadows down side streets, *boots* kicking in the *rain*,

while *wishing* for your roses but *vexed* that they grew

such *willing* thorns while waiting for day to refrain

the night, and night to open up your *gracious* arms

under a Milky Way of *spacious* smiles,

My calendar *well* marked, recycles *stored* alarms,

reminding that the *killed acceptance* of lost miles

left empty in a crush of sleep *adds* its demands,

sees you through a night's *over-plus* desire,

the bitterness of *unkind riches hide* your hands,

with *sea* wind on your cheeks, draping tousled hair.

Will fingertips reach sparks of personal lightning,

still will you please tell when *you'll* be leaving?

'The Stonehenge Code'

Iconcurchaic Muses' Garland

-Whilst I alone did call upon thy aid,
My verse alone had all thy gentle grace;
But now my gracious numbers are decayed,
And my sick Muse doth give another place.
                    -sonnet 79, Shakespeare

1 Domestic Muse   (136)

She *comes willingly*, keeps *something sweet* in the room

parading *blindly* slides socks to clean hardwood floors,

her twilight hand glides, *reckons* to *fill* the vacuum

and sweeps me off to new *untold-suited* colors.

Her *numbers* counted arc through each bathroom care,

the pivot, back bent waterfall *fulfills* all

loveseat *receipts*, the lingerie despair,

the whirlwind hair *proves* her cleansing wherewithal.

The rich *will still treasure* tomorrow's maids,

domestic muse of *love's* labored emergencies,

dust-deviled mop-tops *numbered* as kitchen aids,

wine vinegar *eases* cleaning contingencies.

She *swears* the house wine *will sweeten* things up,

while *filling* X's sad *love accounting* cup.

2 Muse's Wherewithal   (45)

While filling X's, *sad love* accounting cup,

she pops *melancholy's purge* to spread pure mirth

with seven ways to *oppress* a parasol up,

in frilly *motion slides* of half-shell *death's* rebirth.

A little titillation *abides* to *love* late,

she's up all hours *recounting* her date.

As he *desires* her to be a good mate

she asks, "Is you're *absent presence*, not second rate?"

One day *assured* as supernatural,

the next with *embassies tenderly* domestic,

she may cite her *messengers* as factual

while scouring the kitchen *sink*, a mystic.

A fool can see why my *health* thrives as I groom,

when her wherewithal feeds *gladly* on dim gloom.

3 New Old Muse   (146)

When her wherewithal *feeds* gladly on dim gloom

is it the thought of *fooled* love *undying*,

that gives her time to *live* in my *short leased* home,

renovate the fading *mansion* she's supplying?

New *charges* old when the old returns *costly* new,

same *body* moved by *excess* picks up the pen,

same spirit finds old light to see new *ends* through

in rooms where the *divine* can shine again.

So like a house these *terms* hold my embrace

like *body* and *soul* held up to displace,

the broken shards *arrayed* reset the space,

feng shui to rest in the *inheritor's* place.

Now all that's mused leads to a *richer* cup,

love's new worth treasures an *hour spent charging* up.

4 Begging the Muse Pretty Please   (39)

Love's new *worth* treasures an hour spent charging up

but *sings* reposing in the ever-realms of youth,

can never see you old, not *praise* you all cracked up,

Winged Victory, smiling *manners* of *love's* new truth.

She *lost* her head, wings smile undaunted in the air,

who pieced her back, *divided live* frozen flight,

she's taking off forever, *separation's* stare,

remaining flurried lashes, wrinkled gown of light

just as the muse's *torment* left for the last *time*,

in *absence* her revealed eternal summer smile,

the long white folds, robe flowing, *entertains* my climb

to carve a marble heart from *single* fleshy trial.

The call of muse's *better part* to test my ease,

no other *proves* as mean, *teaches* pretty please.

5 Black and White Silent Muse   (46)

No other proves as mean teaches pretty *pleas*,

departures from my *mortal eye* sets off the slip.

Through fingers of an open hand, *divisions* seize

uncatchable light's *determined* celluloid grip.

Unreeled so far up field, instant *freedom* replays

to kiss goodbye the all or nothing *crystal eyes*.

She moves a fog bank seizing *clear piercing* days

when drifting away, *denied* my *pleading* request

against *lied verdicts* for the *heart's* desired rise,

horizon mirage covers my *defensive* unrest,

a sparrow billow's *title* over zooming *eyes*,

Fellini's *questing* foot dream-roped, floats to the skies!

Appearances decide the *conquest* of my choice,

restoring *picture* silences with moving voice.

6 Muse's Engagement   (47)

Restoring *picture* silences with *moving* voice,

mused *banquets* register how she's followed.

She *takes* to rescue, then *sigh*, cheer, rejoice,

for days to thread her maze of *painted pictures* sold.

From *heart to heart's* muse, why count loses short

to animate the alma mater's *present* soul?

Pull up the stops before cuts *smother*, abort

love's famished image for the *eye's* control...

let off, *looked* out flat-landed down the road,

she drones goodbyes, the way to lose *yourself* less,

awakened from *leagues*, the *eye's* overload,

the right time now, a *pictured* wedding dress.

She shares *good turns* to sing against the ill at ease

as if she polished up the truest *heart's* new lease.

7 *Righteous Muse* (48)

As if she polished up the *truest* heart's new lease,

with varied loves that *took* him to the knees,

broke up the gathered garlands, *pleasured* to please

he shakes them down *locked* to her *breast* for handsome fees.

The muse that circulates through him and *stays*,

even when he's *prey* on the lost highway,

discovers what's *best of* the *dearest vulgar* craze,

in guises of extended *worth* she wings *away*.

To rise above canal cliffs to *trust* in her

the *better* part of valor's *greater* battle,

down *jeweled* avenues unwound to recover

love's *gentle thief proves* her *comfort's trifle*.

The *stolen* line's *closure* bares jungles of remorse,

her challenge audits a righteous *grievous* divorce.

8 *Loveseated Muse*   (49)

Her challenge *audit*s a righteous grievous divorce,

strange finger paintings, several scenes spread in vain,

poor arms, not surreal enough to discourse

from all *alleged* angles of cubist portrait pain.

At arms length, the *hands* could not enfold her way,

part vanishing *time* in embracing lines,

two point perspective, her *utmost* Vieux Carre,

iconcurchaic haunts in shaded *sun* confines,

with highlights, *reared up* rhyming, lighter than touch,

more personal than this *converted* outburst

that *scarcely* edges silent lips, would make me blush

to over take her will's *gravitational* thirst.

Though furnished, my defects on her *loveseat* of arts,

ensconced, her distance lies spread through these *part's*.

9 Painting the Muse   (137)

Ensconced, her distance lies spread through these *part's*,

draws black and white, colorful *blind* spots gray,

the space around us *anchored* as light departs,

Night Blooming Jasmine *forged* her *plot's* wordplay.

I waited *widely* framed for her next *world* move

into a shadowed *truth* squeezed from a tube,

the hand's *eye transferred* scanning for the groove,

marked pensive *falsehood*, Rube Goldberg's rude cube.

Corrupted by the muse, *foul* challenged till confused,

my *soul* machine shows her departures as entered,

a studio's *fair truth*, *worst* bliss reused,

the way forms from lines *common* and splintered.

I paint the loss *my erring eye* can't deny

on canvas networked from *my better judgment's eye*.

10 Love Interest Muse   (138)

On canvas networked from my *better* judgment's eye,

pulled back on subtle stretchers, muse *swearing* manners

as if all *flattered* into a sonnet's sky

to serve us well, with what *lies she* tells of treasures.

My ragged *credit* of poor poetic verse

trusts wages of a spendthrift *lover's* heart

to pay transactions each *day* twice in reverse

and *credit simple* interest as they depart.

She booked to *suppress* outstanding accounts,

forgave the debt's *unjust habit* and paid the rest.

I cashed out for her *love's default* amounts,

vowed *vainly* to even loss, seven fold invest.

She paid my *thinking* debt, *believed untutored* heart's

love bails her *truth's* income tax of the arts.

11 *The New Model Muse*   (50)

Love bails her truth's income tax of the arts,

and stages acts to *spur* a *provoking* deal

as *measured*, the muse uncovers artful parts

with charming *grief* of *instinct* none can steal.

As Lady Merlot *eased* a glass of charms

her silk robe rippled for *miles* pouring out

a liquefaction *spurring* art alarms,

my heavy plod answered with a *riding* shout.

The *thrusting* brushes that charge up a canvas,

to catch the muse *reposed*, not throw her back like trout

or *teachers* who skim from less than genius

the muse's surface *journey*, can't do more than tout.

When hunger *weighs* on art to inhale the sky,

the muse *speeds travel's end* to frantic asking why.

The muse speeds travel's end to *frantic* asking why

preserving art's new *angry ill* connections,

I'd paint more than red *hell* in her stone eye

while chipping out *love's desperate prescriptions.*

Where's work where I do not see her *curing* hands

secure with *fair approval* on her face,

how does *truth's* foot fall then rise where she stands,

not *longing* Florentine, in *midnight's* Paris chase?

American flag bleeds, *physicians* her *desire,*

stage set with bare trees for *disease's sickly* pace,

the *fever* of *hell* heavy feet stepping higher,

passed vain care she came, out *reasoned* empty space.

Caught up in *mad* pros and cons of her *past* sting,

her liberties bear *death as dark night's* diamond ring.

13 *Everything about the Muse*   (51)

Her liberties *bear* death as dark night's diamond ring,

as she *speeds* through glass without cracking it,

or when *returning* delays at border crossing

she interrupts the *beast* to stay and interpret.

In honor of her there's no *willful* mistakes,

in how too seek improvement *mounted* along.

She's ready to give me what *jaded* wine talk takes,

clicks glasses high, *excused* when never wrong.

She stands ready to out *pace* documentaries,

muse *mounted on the wind, racing* to resolve

accounts, *desire's perfect* mercenaries,

at issue slippery math, spells what human *loves* solve.

She could make a thing *desired* from nothing,

her loss would key *extremities* of everything.

Her loss would *key* extremities of everything

and alter with impediments the *special* clues

when love's *rich hope* reaches love *unfolding,*

her *instant* removal would *blunt* what *renews.*

The patient love my muse fixed on *long hours*

when ruined *time* demands a lasting stand,

has double gravity's *placed* holding powers,

leaves love's deeper *treasure set* in my hand.

The muse *surveys,* sings of ages that pass

rare faces wearing *wardrobes* shaken to the bone,

who render unknowns seen in light's *jeweled* glass,

no *fine points locked* there *will not* etch in *stone.*

When peering through the night she *hides* the gloom,

she *comes willingly, keeps* something *sweet* in the room.

15 The Muse's Garland

She comes willingly, keeps something sweet in the room,

while filling X's sad love accounting cup.

When her wherewithal feeds gladly on dim gloom,

love's new worth treasures an hour spent charging up.

No other proves as mean, teaches pretty pleas,

restoring picture silences with moving voice

as if she polished up the truest heart's new lease,

her challenge audits a righteous grievous divorce.

Ensconced, her distance lies spread through these part's,

on canvas networked from my better judgment's eye.

Love bails her truth's income tax of the arts,

the muse speeds travel's end to frantic asking why.

Her liberties bear death as dark night's diamond ring,

her loss would key extremities of everything.

II Romantic Dialects & Odes

Full many a thought uncall'd and undetain'd,

And many idle flitting phantasies,

Traverse my indolent and passive brain,

As wild and various as the random gales

That swell and flutter on this subject Lute!

And if all of animated nature

Be but organic Harps diversely frame'd,

That tremble into thought, as o'er them sweeps

Plastic and vast, one intellectual breeze,

At once the Soul of each, and God of all?...

The Incomprehensible! save when with awe

I praise him, and with Faith that inly feels;

Who with his saving mercies heal'ed me,

A sinful and most miserable man,

Wilder'd and dark, and gave me to possess

Peace, and this Cot, and thee, heart-honoured Maid!

--S.T. Coleridge, The Eolian Harp, lines 39-64

Love's Upside Down Crown: Last Rush to First Blush

(for P. H.)

1 Love Contracted on the Hunt (54)

Until one *lives full* where *truth's* counterfeit departs

there's no *fair* hope that *beauty's beauty* has arrived.

All hope springs through now and then, *summer* restarts,

meets with ravaged *masked* contingencies revived.

The cruel if and when *disclosed,* conceived harsher how,

all previous *sweet* love *deaths* gone lead to this,

to celebrate this new *virtue,* here and now,

the world again rounded-out with the *sweetest* kiss.

To dare our fateful dream's *distilled* first pleas

to grant love's twin, love's *tinctured* inoculations

against the world's towering *wonton* miseries,

carries guaranteed love-sick *thorny* conditions.

The end of one does not cure love's *deep dyed* disease,

there is not yet for us tender *beauteous* ease.

2 Retreating from the Hunt   (55)

My *gilded* love verse, not the same as slain before,

once more we have love's *outlived time* of year

when mockingbirds sing as *powerful* but more

in darkness rapt till rendered *brightly* clear.

Fear hidden shadows of *war* survive,

hearts double back, *work out* bird's eye view hours,

impatient, loved alone, *oblivious* alive,

until the darkness breaks from the shadow's *powers*.

That day you meant to let go, *overturn* my hand

as you held it last, stayed to say a *room's* goodbye

then turned again to face me take your *ending* stand,

with *eyes* I could not read you said be *still,* don't lie.

For better *worlds paced* lovers *praise* to raise their hearts

until one *lives* full where truth's counterfeit departs.

3 Returning to the Hunt   (139)

To *justify* the eye a *glancing power* tells,

look back through many rooms where *love* still stares,

pressed over streets and landscapes, ocean swells,

then traveled out, flown *elsewhere* to how she cares

for new *defenses,* loving how we bring

a *cunning* sense to prosper, *empower* it all,

bear up our fleeting hours together, a ring

of constancy to *pains* however small.

Long *wounded* times cursing the evil phone,

prevented outright *kindness*, being mine,

well knowing its *excuse* keeps us, ours alone,

so certain you cannot *kill* its abiding sign

and realize as three years turn *aside* to four

my gilded love's versed not the same as *slain* before.

4 · Retrieving Manners (140)

Wise life becomes all its *cruel press* seeks to be,

the tiger sun and steady *tongue-tied* breeze.

If love's undone and kept under the sea-*sick* sea

it pushes racing waves *expressed* in twos and threes,

a *pity-wanting* beach reappears ahead,

two paths diverge to where a *world* bends without end.

Well traveled *manners* at each wheel's axel-bed

leads back to where *sorrow* came from around the bend.

This day, the year's *mad* time, the miles apart,

survives the backed-up doubt *despaired grown* fears,

our beating as one *slandered testy heart*

conspired to face *mad ears* with *proud* unbridled tears.

When *love disdains* the darting *pain* joy swells

physicians know the *wit* of *health* that *tells*.

5 *Hunting Each Other* (56)

Sweet love, my *love* has never left your side,

though gone *again*, warm strange fleeting *sad* bright,

slow fast yes *today*, now new the feeling's slide,

long lost all past but little mourning, *sharp appetite.*

Loud city sounds crude *force* harsh *edge* quick cut across

deep sober somber heartbeat, *blunter wish, more rare,*

fresh found age-old, *perpetual* wine-gloss loss

moves closer, cold dry darkness, *hunger* seen fear

haunts lone souls, enshrouds the *eye* and its tried mind,

contracted senses, *fullness* never tasted *day,*

dull spirit strained, weeps to *see again* the last kind

unreal real word, you wait for *parted shores* to say.

You *care* to stay, *tomorrow* you *love*, *love* me,

wise life becomes all its cruel press seeks to *be.*

6 Hunting Together (148)

Should we tend tigers too hot for *love's* taming

inspired to hunt more game? A *censured judgment* smile,

the gaze to track fair love lifts that spot, *false* charming

ways your *eyes* stream into mine *watching* for a mile,

breathtaking run *with tears* by river's rapid flow,

no marveled hand till your hand *loves* as if my own

to find pulse blended *mistakes* together, we know

vexed loneliness ends in each one alone.

This captured moment, days parted, *heavens* recede,

as we held off our lost *correspondence* chill.

Dark avenues of stark *world's* admitted need.

I've walked, dissolved in nothingness, *fled* until

you know, the certain footfalls in *faults* can not hide

my *love*. *No*, my *love* has never left your side.

7 Prancing to the Hunt   (57)

There is *not* yet for us *tender* beauteous ease

that ripened years of *desired* loving gives,

we rather share a wishful *service* to please,

an end to searching where the *foolish* heart lives

when everything out *chides the bitter* wherewithal,

a little while of *sovereign* walking in the sun,

to *bid* our *world-without-end-hour clock's* call

then lie received and peaceful, *precious* when it's done.

Right here we *dare* this beautiful imprisoned wild

exotic feral thing which we *slave* to have pinned,

in innocence of a doe-eyed stray *jealous* child

that thirsts, for *absent* fountain drinks at river's bend.

We'll loosen *will's affair* together, *no* blaming,

should we *tend* tigers too hot for *love's* taming.

A Ballad for La Belle Orleanna

Her Creole smile, perma-transient vibes,

Spanish arches, Gothic Clark Gables,

Mercury streets, architectural fables,

Archaic faces with tomorrow's headlines…

With antebellum charm, ghostly alarms,

December morning fog after snowfall swarms,

On her gypsy river a paddle wheeler plays

Songs from the ancient gallery of slaves…

Who could rhapsodize her mystery lines?

Moody cowboy egos under dueling oaks,

Pistols aplenty, unusual shadows,

Beautiful peace of the unknown deceased

Whipped up and blown through the gulf of destiny.

Hip-hop till they drop in a burst of flames,

Guntown tongues cracking bullwhips and chains,

Who could take ten rounds and not go insane,

Shadow boxing the enemies of fame?

Her hurricane ways, improvisational plays

Lead you to a promising swampland,

Will it be your Waterloo, or a fleur-de-lis tattoo?

She invites you to waltz with the wetlands band.

Egyptian ruins enshrine Canal Street,

Cheops walks corridors of midnight

Preparing for Thoth in the choke-hold light,

A museum-ed Atlantis yet to fall,

Who could stop her entombing them all?

When she rings her evacuation bells,

Tolling freedom out before the water swells,

Monarch butterflies and sacred oak trees

Dance and land on her cypress knees.

La belle Orleanna of the wetlands,

plantation mapped plans, true south compass

For the melting pot in her hands.

Who'll measure the scope of her men, woman?

Outside the gulls blue cathedral

The walls like wings open the heights,

At home in the nights purple gold green light

To meld with the majesty of flight.

Sunsets moonstruck on a solstice altar,

The winged grail's unwavering angel star,

Napoleon's Code glides the courtyard tonight

For Leonardo's floor planned mansion twilight.

With a ghost-like moon in the Passover sky,

Second thought confession, Jesus-cloud looms by,

Voodooed confusion mixed midnight chimes,

Who could live her religion of eternal rhymes?

After pondering wild blue bayous

She hides you in strange quarters, torn asunder,

Safe in Andrew Jackson's arms again

At the Gold Mine Bar with a pirate's grin.

La belle Orleanna of the wetlands,

Her eyes of storm see peace surpassing,

Her hurricane ways, improvisational plays,

The grand marina mother of the missing…

Will she offer them to you,

Will it be your Waterloo, or fleur-de-lis tattoo,

The mapped out plans, south compass true,

To measure the wetlands like Bellocq's nudes…

She invites you to waltz at the Wetlands Ball,

La belle Orleanna takes your hand,

leads you to a promising swampland,

La belle Orleanna of the wetlands.

Diva Demoed in my Dream   (58)

Auditioned in a *pardoned* dream one night,

a shadowy woman's *pleasure* to caress,

my back in a dim room on a valley's *strong* light,

green trees, wheat fields to *privilege* my distress.

The touch *bound waiting* for her viola waist,

a musical *vassal strayed* from deeper gloom,

forbidden bodies close, naked turned then faced,

what we embraced *imprisoned* in that room.

While *patiently* noticing her fretting grasp,

the *time tamed* instrument held in her arms,

my neck from whispered breath to *suffered* rasp,

encountered *controls* of her duet charms.

When higher *will* ramped up the register's repair,

in *leisure* on the bed she *craved* our music there.

The Music Room Goddess Dance   (59)

A goddess dance, *beguiling* innumerable arms,

her marble slap, *bare* pattering encoded feet,

inventions not far from battles, the city street,

composes air for instruments, blends with her charms

in whirling power *formed* universal joy,

revolving call to youth for the *former boy*

who turned *five hundred* orbits back to hers,

sweet boy who got away from *antique* monsters.

Old records search the *world* for pinnacles of bliss

as toes *course* under *wonderful* knee bends!

How could he love her less in *backward looks* from this,

to where the goddess grants the dance of *framed amends*?

The contemplated *revolution* goddess gazed

spins by humanity she *admires* as she's *praised*.

Chiaroscuro Dream through Sunglasses   (61)

Her *waking* sigh stirred with the river's *tenor*

from banks that held the bridge for her *slumbers,*

Pavane guitars *replayed* in *heavy* waver

suspended notes *rest* her *deeds idle hours.*

Above *desire's shamed* high girded towers,

mock engineered architecture, *watching* sculpture,

imagined far from home scoping flowers

in *jealous* zones of future Renaissance culture,

chiaroscuro *watches,* secret tattooed tongue,

mixed media *night's* fleeting *shadows broken,*

defeated past colors, the *watchman* young,

peers new horizons as mornings *open.*

The tidal moon times *waking* for *elsewhere's* mark,

shines constantly *off* backgrounds *ever* dark.

A Wandering Bark's Bliss

Life raft encased guitar came and I tuned

myself into the rescue of her sound.

The echo on my lap, strange chords returned,

till inner ears stood octaves upside down.

Her cedar cypress blended avenue,

to guide me led into a starry field's repose,

a passage of two ships joined in the blue,

a wandering bark whose path cuts through the blows

on calm and stormy seas, to neck heel checked,

gapped tight twelfth fret, each string struck to the nib,

the hands on deck chime mermaids to collect

love songs of first heard sirens lured from the jib.

Her aria caught up as deep frets replied

with overtones, invited her bliss to be plied.

Country Girl in a Small Town Bar   (142)

A bayou wind fans the *ground* as she aims

to take prize money with a *scarlet* twirl

while dancing the *ornamental* bikini games,

from kitchens of country delights, fine *rooted* girl.

Stepped from a luxury car's *revenue* surprise

to little bar with whiskey river *beds* on ice,

she stalks the floor with *pitiless* tiger *eyes*,

small town *virtue*, Louisiana Cajun cries.

Give her room to lean a *loving* dream on,

parted lush *lips* pretty as her *pity* smiles,

unsealed moves to loose *bonds* of imagination,

deserving example free-winging on the tiles.

Would she care to sing, *rent* Fred Jung's band, Pink Freud,

profoundly *compare* with the musically annoyed?

Guest House   (62)

In my *possession's* pride her welcomed quote,

would want my *remedy* for an ambulance,

as if to strum a peaceful slumber's *beaten* note,

guitar parts *gracious* to her intimate offense.

Would pierced ears *account* for rosebuds in dismay

as my notes pick and *chop* buds of darling May

replanted in *antiquity's* current dark clay,

steel strings gripped on a winter's iconic *day*?

While picking at her garden's grace note *grounded* needs,

contrary to improvisational traction,

bouquets of melodies pulled *iniquity's* weeds,

from *aged* rooms in her Creole gardened mansion.

Her welcome sign's *surmounted* trestle blossomed spring,

concealed the *inward* thorns she *shaped*, forced me to sing.

Grandma's Portrait   (149-150)

When grandma died, the hill *took on* her portrait,

a shade *frowned* on her shadow curving with the wind,

a *tyrant* river's *power* swept her hair straight

beside the *hated* road that killed her at the bend.

Revenge for her *swayed* back left leafless in the night,

commanded fire *eyes*, jewels in a velvet glove.

She grew plush that spring, *bright blind* in full *daylight*,

rain's *motion* posed the presence of mother's love.

The wintering oak's *mighty state*, landscape's refuge,

had *warranted* the tangents of a branched out life,

bomb-choked survivor's *mind* flashed to full surge,

the *motion's* hillside orchard *merited* new wife.

One sunset *served* an autumn *defect* in her face,

abhorrent to her profile on the ridgeline's trace

where I once walked and *fawned* as a child by her side

to castle garden's where she never roamed *despised*.

Mother's Spirit   (63)

They each took turns and curled *against* her side

as she lay on her last bed's *time* to fly,

her sons and daughters, one by one *fortified*

by her goodness, their goodness to *fortify*

as she lay *vanishing* to take the sky

to welcome *beauty's* liberated spirit,

receive her *travel* well to shrouded cloud's bright eye,

embraced with *age*, her sacred *King* to clear it.

A soul's *sweet* child returned to her children

from end to end, *love's* unending *sight* that bends

back through them over *memory* back again,

as steady, *never cut*, what *love* contends.

You'll want her there in your last *hour's* descent,

to brush the *lines and wrinkles* out, shake up ascent.

Past Life Regression   (64)

Has your past life regressed, *defaced* to change you much,

how would friends know a *rich-proud* difference in you,

your reach in books achieve a *lofty* deeper touch,

razed purgatory daisies from a rearward view

to see the stem-sets round *immortal* crown of green

hold petals placed like blades of a *kingdom* machine

till it propels you back to this exact *aged* place

seen through same eyes from a distant *watery* face

instead of straight forward raptured *interchanged* gaze,

return to that dark room's *decayed* far corner door

and grasp the knob *confounded* till it turns once more,

cracks open as you peer *away* old light through haze,

eternal slave to your chosen *death*-slept soul,

poured back into your new cracked *weeping* bowl?

Blue Brilliance   (68)

She led me to a shelf of books that *mapped her days*

like suitors offering *flowers* for her tables,

at windows where the loveseat cushioned her *true* ways

by two French Quarter *antique* courtyard fables.

Her raven hair draped *summer's* voluminous verse,

lip parted *cheeks*, jet black *tresses* shamed rose petals,

her teeth and eyes glinted *ornamental* sharpness

that softened lights, her *inhabited* miracles

incanting deeper rarities *lived* to finesse.

I sat and savored braver *outworn* opulence,

in firm folds of the *robbing* page's trembling trance,

a *sepulcher* opened, blossomed in my abyss.

When path webbed *hours* of *holy* tangle

crossed *beauty's* edge cleared from deepest jungle,

to *map* the butterfly's Blue Royal *green* union,

passed Unicorn Orchids, *signs* to Rose of Sharon,

the rock that's hewn and *dressed* by no human hand,

new transits multiplied, atmospheric facets,

hurls *nature's* great domed crystal towers through the land,

blue-jeweled sky *fleece*-clouds spread new to *golden* planets.

All Along There   (69)

We traveled out our lives, this *far* away to *mind*

returned beginnings from *world* ends so kind,

when hearing *praise*, she'd rather *eye* my *outward* sway

till such a *voice* there blossomed *bare* to her big day.

Her rooms of *mended* shelter *guesses* to confide,

enfolds mixed *measures* to *confound* our orphan tide.

When our tree's wracked and fallen, *uttered flowers* gone,

we'll *grow* a tree-house *ranked* up by an August moon

for sweet *soul truth* to *bare tongues* without a spar,

accents amused, *thoughts farther* than La Chat Noir.

You'll wonder in *due* days, *commend* where this came from

when *curled* through the door as *crowned* you can't yet come.

What's left from pure *soiled beauty*, you to me in song,

it happened once as *common, praised* there all along.

A Queen's Review (for Maxine)   (65)

Her spirit writes the better part of her *power*

consuming light, her words long *mortal* composure,

the other side of sleep, *beauty* waking over

dreams flowing shades deep, double *wracked* exposure.

The dual *day*, word-winded *restful* prescient breath,

like smoke rises, a *honey* consciousness incense.

Her words refuse *impregnable* ravages, death,

with montage eye, rye rabbi, suspense *black ink* sense.

Her poems, a mother's well prepared *jeweled* nest,

for milking kindness nurtured *time-chest* waterlines.

Her eyes shined *meditation's* philosopher test,

wisdom's gemstones of eternal *miracle* signs.

Unburdened by death, lines dig, *decay*, exhume,

replant the love of her words, *shine bright* to full bloom.

Will's Way   (144)

When settled up with *pride*, to write my *comfort's* will

determining *two* willed *sides* of *spirit's* estate,

my will accordingly will, *till good angels still*

the spacious *angel* will's *telling* amalgamate.

If your will's *purity* accepts my will's *worse* ways

to count the *rightful* number of my will as *two*,

when our wills *turn one* from what *tempts* and strays,

your will will *love* my *despair* if mine *corrupts* you.

Not knowing how you will *direct* my *suspect* self,

my will *fires* yours to arrange *both* for abundance,

suggests another volume's well-willed *colored* shelf

with *hell's* will covered, binding reason's *fiendish* chance.

When my will *fairs* well, wooing *saints* acceptably,

your will may *doubt* will's *better angel out* of me.

A Sect of One (*Plus One*)   (143)

Lo, hoped for human muse, mentor the *mothered* gun

your life had stood, a harbinger *creature's* touchstone,

a talisman's *reprise*, Jung's *running* "sect of one,"

her words *cried* sermon, transcendental Dickinson.

Inclusion in a double-*catch dispatch* with *you*,

to know *you* in the carriage *pursuit* next *to me*,

two couplets *hold your neglected* garden in view,

the horse heads neigh *bent* to *face* the oak and posy.

The circled coming *stay*, forever *busy* full,

entirely for Shakespeare, *crying* in constraints,

where revelations *chase*, ours *fly* the *back turned* tool,

behold *me*, next to *you*, *kiss me*, one of *your* saints.

To stanza-land we hurry, *pray* for *Will's* same *care*,

your bearings *catch* us to the airless *turn* we'll share.

This antique book *returns* to some psalm's grace

when *bent* to each one, ambient to each ones place

as written in the quick of a *catching* heart,

not far *behind* words *prayed* to *quicken* future art.

The *child-like* hand that curved a holy specter's mind,

two point perspective into the future shined,

whether troubadour's *loud* warble or David's tale

unbound to *chase* the secret in the thunder's bell,

until the shepherd's flocks through new madrigals *fly*,

embrace her *housewife cares, kind face* with my eye.

ASAP: Age of Second Adam's Paradigm

The wings of birds in flight, the ideal smile

of Leonardo's resurrected pointing John,

the finger painted Mona's, never out of style,

reveals self-knowledge, mirrors ones prison archon.

Preparing for the final conflict's cosmic seam,

Blue Turbaned Prince, Iran's devouring Beast,

twilight adjunct time, twixt waking thought and dream,

angelic blessing for the coming written feast.

A six-string medley of three songs cascade,

to tall oaks as their inner flight rose in song,

a choir of birds chiming flourishes as I played,

a sect of one's oracle lifting me along.

Passed winged words parting on a razor's edge

while contemplating angels from a mountain ledge

who travel deep in valleys for a second look

between the pages fading of a mission book,

the end returns Pleroma's unfallen fullness,

to find us resting there in perpetual bliss.